School Days 101

Dr. Angela Farmer

Kendall Hunt
publishing company

Cover image © Shutterstock.com

Kendall Hunt
publishing company

www.kendallhunt.com
Send all inquiries to:
4050 Westmark Drive
Dubuque, IA 52004-1840

Copyright © 2017 by Dr. Angela Farmer

ISBN 978-1-5249-1268-0

Kendall Hunt Publishing Company has the exclusive rights to reproduce this work,
to prepare derivative works from this work, to publicly distribute this work,
to publicly perform this work and to publicly display this work.

All rights reserved. No part of this publication may be reproduced,
stored in a retrieval system, or transmitted, in any form or by any
means, electronic, mechanical, photocopying, recording, or otherwise,
without the prior written permission of the copyright owner.

Published in the United States of America

This is dedicated to the people who have always
kept me focused on what really matters,
Max, Grant, and Claire
To the Moon and Back, Times Infinity

And to my husband, Scott, my biggest fan,
AF

School Days 101: Lessons for Lifelong Learners

This book provides an introduction to many of the issues critical to education today. I hope you will find the advice and insight to be useful in your journey, both personally and professionally. With ample devotion and determination, education truly can become the toughest job you'll ever love.

Contents

Introduction	ix
Kindergarten Readiness?	1
Imagination: The Key to Learning	4
Reimagining the School Week	7
The Value of Playtime	10
Now I Lay Me Down to Sleep	13
Zero Tolerance Examined	16
Redshirting Kindergarten	19
Dyslexia Discussed	22
Just Say No to Zeros	25
On the Road Again	28
Semester Stress	31
Demystifying Differentiation	34
The Real Impact of High School Students Who Work	37
Pre-K for All	40
Reaching for Rigor	43
Apples to Apples?	46
Classroom Management 101	49
Senioritis, Fact or Fiction	52
STEM Growth	55
Now You See Them...	58
Customer Service, P-12 Style	61
Out of the Box	64
The Value of a Routine	67
The Ungraded Primary	70
Lefties Unite	73
Farewell to the Bell	76
Learning from Lexiles	79
To Friend or Not to Friend	82

Little Uniformity on Uniforms	85
Time on Task	88
Sedentary Secondary Schools	91
Keeping Tabs	94
Communicating with Today's Teen	98
Bibliography	101
Biography	104

Introduction

Education today has evolved far beyond its initial inception of a way to share faith with the masses. It has become a powerhouse of political, social, and economic capital. Unfortunately, those whose labor produces what society truly values in education too often go unnoticed. These pages have been crafted to help share some "boots on the ground" logic, practicality and professionalism in a time where educators are often criticized for doing too little with too few and taking too long to realize quantitative value. The true value of an educated society lies not in the enumerated test score calibrations, but rather in the quality and comprehension realized at the end of the journey by those called to teach. It is not a profession enamored with prestige or power.

It does, however, afford the educator the single most important role played in a child's life other than his parents. It is truly the hand that leads the class that shapes the world. What is communicated both in word and action in classrooms today dramatically influences the opinions, temperament, dedication, and passion with which the next generation will embrace society. There is no more critical calling at than that of shaping tomorrow's leaders to reimagine a way to create a society better than it has been and only the beginning of what it can become, through education, the greatest equalizer of all.

Kindergarten Readiness?

As the school year closes on the end of the last quarter, many schools are conducting Kindergarten readiness inventories. These may be better known as Kindergarten registrations. However, in truth, readiness for Kindergarten involves a great deal more than hitting a chronological marker in order to be age appropriate for school. Being ready for Kindergarten is much more aligned with being ready for matriculation into an industrial setting than simply being 5 years old and ready to play and learn one's colors. Kindergartens in the United States today are designed with a broad set of both learning and behavioral objectives. Gone are gentle preparation programs for school where a few hours of organized learning are softened by a 30-minute nap and some free play.

Today's Kindergartens have been forced to become critical, first step programs to ensure that up and coming first graders are ready for both the academic as well as social-emotional rigors of elementary school. They are the melting pot where

children who did not attend preschool are comingled with those who have been in preschool. Those acclimated to childcare for many years are blended with those who have never been separated from their parents for even the briefest independence.

The challenge for the teacher is daunting. She is required to adapt to each child's intellectual experiences and emotional maturity immediately upon his crossing the threshold of her classroom. Some can read and write and spell and sit for long spans of time quietly. Some cannot recognize any letters, hold a crayon, or sit for the briefest span of time without a dramatic outburst. Others come with English as a second language and cannot initially carry on a conversation. Clearly, differentiation seems a most inane word for the juggling act that an effective Kindergarten teacher must perform from day one of the Kindergarten experience.

Kindergarten readiness means much more today than in years past when chronological readiness meant school readiness. Gone are the days when learning started in Kindergarten. Much is expected of these tiny students when they begin their first big day. It is, in many ways, the end of life as they have known it. It transforms them from babes in arms to students in rows. Much of their readiness for learning is directly related to their maturity not just their age. In order to be ready to learn new things, they must be able to sit, somewhat quietly, and to follow directions reasonably well. They also must be independent enough to take care of their most basic needs and behave nicely, most of the time, to those around them.

Being ready for Kindergarten is serious business. Much is to be learned and applied in a relatively short window of time. Therefore, it is critical that Kindergarten classrooms be equipped with a teacher both empathetic enough to recognize to a variety of needs and talented enough to help them all learn in a somewhat coordinated manner such that, at the end of the year, they are ready, willing, and able to march confidently toward the real world, first grade.

Imagination: The Key to Learning

The 21st century has delivered a number of exciting and revolutionary opportunities for educators in K-12 education regarding digitalized instruction through such companies as Kahn Academy and Virtual Nerd, as well as a plethora of tools and applications that students and teachers can use. According to Bill Frezza's October 1, 2015, interview of Sal Kahn, developer of the Kahn Academy, the format provides a student paced pedagogy which relies heavily on digital media and allows the student to be control of his learning. Unlike a traditional class setting where there are finite,

delivered lectures and the students have to digest (or often regurgitate) the material on demand, Kahn Academy videos allow the students to individually set the pace and frequency of the instruction and reteaching, as necessary. Students taking the modules do not move along until they have mastered the concept, avoiding what the founder calls "Swiss Cheese Learning" (Kahn, 2015).

Virtual Nerd, on the other hand, was developed by graduate students at St. Louis University who recognized that they tutored the same topics over and over (Salcman & Shmeylovich, 2010). They rather softly developed the Virtual Nerd as a presentation and learning format for mathematics understanding in 2008. The company, now owned by Pearson, is also an app that provides on-the-go access to tutorials from middle school to high school math concepts. It has an expanded target audience to encompass students, teachers, and parents. There are online learning workshops, lessons, courses, and entire schools where students are relegated to the virtual world of learning. These tools provide students exponentially greater access to relevant and current data to expand their intellectual curiosity and to go as Star Trek so often referenced "where no *one* has gone before."

What has not evolved at the speed of light are the tools that educators use employ to address the multifaceted nature of digital learning. This leaves educators and educational leaders outside of most adults' comfort zones, having to respond to a stimulus with an appropriate response when the stimulus itself is entirely new. Unfortunately, they, too, must figure out a way to navigate this unchartered territory. The path toward understanding and most effectively adapting to this "Brave New *Digital* World" requires following a new set of practices where lifelong learning requires one to be current on the trends of the trade as well as those that are on the cusp of delivery. Perhaps it is time to analyze the true genius of Albert Einstein's legacy in his famous quote that "Imagination is more important than knowledge." Certainly, no one knows that better than the digital natives of the millennial generation.

Reimagining the School Week

While the traditional school week for Kindergarten-Grade 12 students is recognized as a Monday through Friday structure covering an average of 7 hours, budget constraints and online learning opportunities have necessitated a reimagined week for many districts in the United States. According to the Education Commission of the States published by the University Alliance in 2013, roughly 100 districts in 17 states use 4-day weeks for student instruction as a solution to districts in financial hardships (NACEP Conference Archives, 2013).

While the 4-day school week idea has been around for decades in states like Wyoming and Idaho, Peach County, Georgia, is one of the newest adopters according to Bob Ross at www.Education.com. Representing a community of just under 24,000 citizens, they were faced with a drastic budget shortfall. While few were elated about the initial proposition of the 4-day student week, the possibility of losing 39 teachers frightened the community more, shared Sara Mason, a spokesperson for the school system (Ross, 2010).

In the article published by University Alliance in 2013, the biggest concern is what happens to the students when they are away from the school on that nonattendance day.

Peach County answered that concern with the assistance of the community groups, churches, and nonprofits who helped organize a low-cost day care for parents on the nonattendance day. District statistics from this new week have surprised even the proponents who anticipated mild savings. With Mason citing the cost of substitutes down 76%, transportation down 35%, utility costs down 8%, and student discipline incidents down 40%.

Colorado's Garfield School District trimmed its budget, going to the 4-day school week in 2013 according to an article by Kelsey Sheehy in highschoolnotes@usnews.com (Sheehy, 2013). The move for this rural district amounted to $480,000 in annual savings, realized by reductions in the hours of bus drivers and paraprofessional staff. Hansen School District in Idaho, which moved to the 4-day week in 2010, keeps connected with the students on Fridays by offering scheduled homework help as well as professional development or teachers.

While the University Alliance acknowledges the topic's divisive nature, regardless as to whether it brings welcome or unwelcomed opportunities, many districts may find the 4-day school week as one of the few, remaining options to save operating budgets and maintain quality instruction. Stephen Pruitt, chief of staff for the Georgia Department of Education, says, "I think it's a topic for discussion at a lot of places. I think school districts are going to be looking at all possibilities to save money. If they can do something they feel will not hurt the kids, they will consider it seriously" (Ross, 2010).

The Value of Playtime

To play or not to play, that has become the question. Recognized by Kenneth Ginsburg and the American Academy of Pediatrics as essential to child development, play contributes to the mental, developmental, and social emotional well-being of children (Ginsburg, 2006). However, many children find themselves in a hurried and intensely focused lifestyle that often limits their opportunity for free-play, play that is child driven and devoid of adult instructions (Snow, 2011).

According to a *Psychology Today* article entitled "The Value of Play," the essence of play can be summarized by the following five aspects. It is self-chosen and self-directed. The play activity values the means above the ends, and the rules are created by the minds of the participants. It is unique and imaginary, and it includes an engaged but unstressed mindset (Gray, 2008).

Montana State University's 2010 MontGuide details play in a variety of forms explaining how play evolves over time, including such facets as parallel

play from the age of 18 months to 2 years where children play in a similar setting without interactive play. Social play is explored where children around three begin to interact with others. Expressive play where children interact with tangible materials such as paint and clay. Cooperative play opportunities develop later as preschool age children mature. The outcomes manifest as a leader emerges and children are clearly in or out of the group dynamic (Anderson-McNamee, 2010).

Regardless of the facet of play studied, the research is clear that play and learning are not mutually exclusive entities. Differentiation is detailed by the observation that children given adult instruction will limit themselves to the intended use for a given toy. Conversely, children given the latitude to discover the toy's use found it to be useful for its intended purpose as well as for a variety of other uses and games of imagination, unexplored in the children directed by the adults.

Ultimately, although the world has become a fast-paced and competitive environment for adults, they must be considerate of the fact that children are more than just miniature adults-in-waiting. They are precious and unique individuals learning through play.

Now I Lay Me Down to Sleep

"Now I lay me down to sleep," begins the familiar children's prayer. It is often the first of many strategies used by parents and caregivers alike as they begin the process of getting their children to fall asleep. As simplistic as going to sleep may appear on the surface, when it comes to children and ensuring that they develop regular, adequate sleep patterns, the simplicity quickly becomes essential. There is clear evidence that sleep enhances memory as well as the brain's "neural plasticity," maximizing communication between children's synaptic connections (Kensinger & Payne, 2010). Further the evidence supports that performance in sophisticated tasks employing higher brain functioning is directly impacted by sleep deprivation. Ensuring that children go to sleep and stay asleep is key toward whether they, as infants, develop the cerebral connections for language acquisition and spatial organization needed later in life. The necessity for adequate sleep remains essential throughout childhood and adolescence where children up to 16 years old still physiologically need 9 to 10 hours of sleep nightly.

According to the *British Medical Journal,* children with nonstandard bedtimes, consistently sleeping less than 10 hours per night up until the age of three, are negatively impacted regarding reading aptitude, mathematical skills, and even spatial awareness. Furthermore, this latency continues to impact these children,

resulting in developmental delays, establishing the first 3 years as perhaps the most "sensitive" time during which sleep is critical for brain development (Griffiths, 2013).

In a 2015 study funded by the National Institute of Health and investigated by Washington State University, researchers report that "rapid eye movement or REM sleep converts waking experiences into lasting memories in young brains, while the absence of the REM tends to allow these fragile experiences to be forgotten." One key researcher, Dr. Marcos Frank, explains that young brains go through key phases of plasticity or remodeling. These are the times when vocal, motor, and social skills are developed. He cites the wealth of data regarding the impact that sleep deprivation has on children, negatively impacting their performance in the classroom. Further his study helps articulate why expanding a child's daily sleep pattern is key to facilitating effective learning (Philips, 2015).

Additionally, the 2010 *Science Digest* study addresses adolescent sleep data on exposure to digital media as directly related to decreased sleep quality, validating that "excessive exposure to media negatively impacts sleep, learning and memory in children" (Kensinger & Payne, 2010). As routine an exercise as getting children to sleep may appear, data from researchers across the world support the necessity that adults must ensure children consistently get adequate sleep. For as Robert Rosenberg cites in "Sleep and Childhood Brain Development," "their future may depend upon it" (Rosenberg, 2013).

Zero Tolerance Examined

Without question, school safety is paramount. The manner in which safety is established and maintained, however, is often the subject of much debate. According to the Vera Institute of Justice's December, 2013, brief, Congress required schools to develop "tough-on-crime" policies through the Gun Free School Schools Act of 1994. Many schools adjusted their handbooks to impose stricter consequences, while some districts even established zero tolerance policies designed to maximize student safety. Such measures also ensured that they would continue to qualify for federal funds as the Act required all school districts to "expel any student, for at least one year, who brings a weapon to school" (Subramanran, Moreno, & Broomhead, 2013).

Zero tolerance, however, has become less favorable as districts acknowledge student behavior often requires reason to ensure that the punishment meets the infraction rather than utilizing of a one size fits all mentality. Many districts across the country are reevaluating unilateral policies which were once seen as the only way to address misconduct, especially in high-poverty schools. Unfortunately, the implementation of zero tolerance policies resulted in over two million students suspended annually in grades 9 to 12 (Subramanran, Moreno, & Broomhead, 2013).

Surprisingly, zero tolerance policies in some areas meant that infractions like weapon possession in school buildings as well as nonviolent offenses like tardiness

all warranted suspension or expulsion. According to a 2011 report by the Council of State Governments Justice Center, Texas reported suspending "nearly 60 percent of its students by the time they graduated from high school." This report documents how suspensions and expulsions can foreshadow "poor outcomes for kids," citing low grades and decreased academic performance and an increase in the likelihood of students becoming incarcerated (Fabelo, et al., 2011).

According to researcher Carly Berwick's report, "Administrators don't suspend kids because they love kicking kids out of school. It happens because they don't know what else to do." Adding insult to injury suspending students for minor offenses enforces "obedience more than the kind of independent thinking valued by four-year colleges" (Berwick, 2015).

Clearly, identification of the deficits of zero tolerance cannot be elicited without recognizing that school administrators must have another option. Recommendations from the American Psychological Association's 2006 Task Force Report include applying discipline policies with flexibility, taking into consideration the school context and reserving zero tolerance for only the most egregious behaviors. Furthermore, they recommend using proactive measures to enhance school culture and establish a sense of student identity within that environment. As Berwick reports, "When kids are struggling, it's not that they don't want to learn; it's that they are missing some set of skills, preventing them from learning. . .removing them from the classroom doesn't build those skills" (Reynolds, et al., 2008).

Redshirting Kindergarten

Kindergarten readiness was historically determined by a child's birthday. Children in the 1970s, for example, attended Kindergarten in the calendar year they turned 5 years old. Children with late summer and fall birthdays, as long as they turned 5 by the year's end, were typically sent to Kindergarten. However, much has changed since Kindergarten meant preparing for school versus attending school.

According to "Redshirting: What's It All About?," Kindergarten has evolved from mastery of blocks and paint to handling pencil, paper, books, and playground rules (Williams, 2011). In 2015, this expanded further to include manipulation and interpretation of electronic devices such as iPads, computers, and other handheld tools set to measure and improve cognitive processing. Further challenging Kindergarten entrants is the definition of a Kindergarten day. In 1977, only 28% of schools structured full-day Kindergarten, allowing time for the children to rest and

acclimate to the stresses of school on a less intense scale. By 2013, this number had risen to 77% where full-day programs were mandatory (Moore, Croan, & Wertheimer, 2003). Clearly, the rules have changed.

Faced with the stress and pace set by the new-age Kindergarten, many parents now elect to redshirt their children with the hope that the extra year of preschool will prepare them for the rigors of Kindergarten as well as enhance their athletic prowess when the time comes. Furthermore, in "The Pros and Cons of Holding Out," parents of the late entry Kindergartens are much more likely to then pressure the schools for a more advanced curriculum for their child upon his latent entry into the system (Graue & Smith, 1996) . Redshirting, once used only as a reference to high school and college athletes to enhance their athletic edge given another year to grow and mature, has now stepped down to the ranks of Kindergarten. The Center for Education Statistics reported that in 2011, nearly 10% of all Kindergarten-age children were redshirted with the majority representing boys.

However, according to research of 8,500 Wisconsin students, holding back revealed no difference in academic advancement for the redshirted Kindergarteners versus their traditional aged peers (Graue & Smith, 1996). Notably, they did report that redshirts were 1.89 times more likely to participate in special needs programs. When comparing retainees to redshirts, a key pattern was noted. Retainees, children held back due to inadequate academic performance, were more likely to be children of color living in poverty whose parents could not afford an additional year of preschool versus the redshirts, whose parents intentionally held them back to prepare more for that first big step into Kindergarten.

To send their children to Kindergarten on pace or later in the race is a dilemma faced by many parents. There are no definitive steps that guarantee success; however, with substantial numbers of parents now opting to redshirt that first year, it definitely begins to blur the lines of what is meant and expected of one to be a Kindergartener.

Dyslexia Discussed

Dyslexia, also called specific reading disability, is recognized in children when they experience marked difficulty in the ability to convert written letters to speech. While it is a common cause in children who experience difficulty in reading, it is surrounded by a vast array of misinformation.

The Yale Center for Dyslexia identifies several of the most common myths (dyslexia.yale.edu, n.d.). The most common fallacy is that dyslexic children all write letters and words backward. While all children learning to read and process language may write letters or words backward in an effort to learn to write them independently, dyslexic children do not write backward with more frequency than other children. Another frequent statement is that all dyslexic children are boys. The reality is that dyslexic diagnoses are split nearly evenly between the genders. Many parents also initially expect that their child will grow out of dyslexia. Dyslexic children's brains simply process the steps of learning to decode letters and words differently. It is an alternative processing, not a developmental delay nor does it indicate any latency in cognitive ability.

There are *10 Things Parents Need to Know to Help a Struggling Reader* (Jenkins, n.d.). The primary action is to focus on the child's strengths. Second, is to celebrate every success, for example, high-five each other for every new word he decodes or self-corrects. Setting realistic goals is also key. Expecting a dyslexic child to read on grade level within a short window of time is unrealistic. Sharing personal difficulties is also recognized as essential for the child to realize that no one is good at everything. Read aloud to children with dyslexia is highly recommended as is understanding of the content. Parents are encouraged to reinforce their support so the child realizes that he is not judged for being different. Establishing small steps toward larger goals of reading comprehension is key. Finally, accepting a slower reading pace while empowering the child to advocate for himself, asking the teacher for more time, or help deciphering a particular text are critical to his progress.

Parents concerned that their child may have dyslexia, should talk to their child's teacher as soon as they suspect a problem. Generally, a Speech Language Pathologist can diagnose dyslexia. Together with the team of educational experts, parents can learn how to best support their child's specific reading disability and ensure that he learns to read and process written material in a manner most conducive to his individual learning pattern.

Just Say No to Zeros

Effective student assessments provide accurate feedback for the teacher as well as the student. A student who scores a 90, for example, provides feedback to the teacher that the concepts were effectively communicated and that some learning occurred. The 90 also communicates to the student that he has mastered the content he learned. There are a number of tools that provide detailed feedback regarding student learning. Some of the most effective include item analysis, reteaching, and differentiation. A punitive zero is not one of those tools.

According to "The Case Against the Zero," traditional grading scales that use 4, 3, 2, 1, and 0 for A, B, C, D, and F are very different from the 100-point scale used in the vast majority of assessments. For example, using a 10-point scale of 90, 80, 70, and 60, an F would equate to a 50. Giving a student a zero for work worth 100 points "asserts that work that is not turned in deserves a penalty many times form severe than that assessed for work that is done wretchedly and is worth a D" (Reeves, 2004). Furthermore, when the 100-point scale uses zeros as penalty

grades, for whatever the reason, the statistical impact is the same as if a negative 6 is used on a 4-point scale.

In additional but aligned research entitled, "Grading: What's the problem with giving zero's?" the author asserts that "zero's do not teach, but–even more importantly- zero's on the 100 point scale are de-motivators to students and their learning" (Foekler, 2012). The students quickly realize that just two zeros are typically all that is required for a student to fail an entire semester. Thomas Guskey, in "Zero Alternatives" asserts that "one would hope that teachers would not use a zero as a weapon, but it still occurs" (Guskey, 2004). He further notes that those using zeros as a weapon are "missing the importance of grading that reflects student learning."

Alternatives to zeros require developing a grading system using "thoughtful and deliberate decisions about the purpose and manner of grading" according to Guskey. One of the best alternatives is incomplete grades, which require students to complete an assignment in another setting and time with the teacher available to further support the student's efforts. This doesn't let students "off the hook" like a zero, and it further reinforces the reason for the grades. Preparing students for the real world, lessons learned are also devoid of zeros. For example, if one were to fail his driving test, would he never be allowed to attempt again? No, additional attempts are allowed until such point as either the novice driver passes or he is enrolled in a driving school setting to acclimate himself with the protocols and rules of the road.

Zeros are neither productive nor inspirational and most often then ensure an irreversible breach of trust between the student and the teacher. Mistakes happen, good teaching is about effectively empowering and assessing student learning not about using zeros as punitive punishment for noncompliance.

On the Road Again

As most drivers have no doubt noticed, schools are back in session. Even without a P-12th grade student in one's home, he couldn't miss the barrage of big, yellow buses transporting students to and from their scholastic destinations. With 480,000 school buses on the road each day, transporting 26 million students annually, the American School Bus Council undoubtedly oversees "the largest mass transportation fleet in the country," (National School Transportation Association, 2013).

While there appears to be no end in sight for the need to transport students regularly, many things have changed in the evolution of school bus transportation. For example, many states have amended distances students must live from the school in order to receive transportation to reduce both the number of routes as well as the number of students transported. Further, the school buses themselves have undergone a metamorphosis. Newer, more efficient buses have replaced vintage transportation models which offered little more than covered transportation

down jarringly rough terrain. Many newer models offer air conditioning, improved seatback protection, security camera support, and WiFi. If such improvements seem like unjustified expenses, one might consider traversing generous lengths of road, down highway and byway, through ill-kept lanes for hours at a time with 65 students seated 3 to a seat. Many student bus routes are in excess of an hour each way. Even with these added amenities, it's a long, tough road to drive a bus and often a long, crowded seat in which to ride one.

In addition to the roughly 65 students that most buses are "capable" of transporting, one must also take into account the baggage that students are required to bring with them on a daily basis to add to the weight and internal congestion of the bus. A given group of 7th graders, for example, are likely to sit 3 to a seat, each of them carrying a large backpack stuffed with books and binders, a musical instrument, and a lunchbox. In the winter months, the togetherness increases further with the addition of bulky, winter coats.

There is little doubt that a good deal of a child's peer rapport is gleaned from the topics addressed on the miles of terrain between home and school. Amid this social acclimation, it is paramount that children be able to board buses, confident that other drivers are both cognizant and courteous to the bus itself, as well as to the students embarking and disembarking on their journey home. In addition to the daily challenges of driving any given vehicle, bus drivers must navigate the routes with the compounded responsibility of ensuring the safety and security of other people's children. Accolades and commendations for each and every person who has every found himself behind the wheel of a school bus. It is truly other drivers' responsibility to be aware and alert. School buses are on the road again.

Semester Stress

This is the season for students across the nation to feel the stresses of semester examinations. Rather a newly minted high school student or a seasoned college graduate student, final examinations are nothing to take lightly. The stress of being assessed for one pinnacle grade which, in many cases, poses a serious impact to a student's overall GPA adds further to the stress of attempting to recall topics and issues and situations posed months before, when the ideas were young. With more than 85% of students feel stress during semester exams (Andruss, n.d.), there are clearly a number of proven, positive, proactive steps that students can take. According to "10 Ways to Make Sure You Survive End-of-Semester Stress," (Wright, n.d.) students should do the following:

- Make a schedule-when are the exams?
- Make lists of things to do–include in these things you may need.
- Take "brief" breaks–just long enough to refocus not long enough lose a day.

- Eat well–healthy foods with high protein and lots of water are key.
- Sleep–total deprivation of sleep is never a good thing.
- Get started early–the best part of the day to study can be captured before noon.
- Partner up–a study partner is a great way to master content.
- Ask questions–question other students, teaching assistants, and teachers.
- Look at old assignments–any related assignments can access can offer insight.
- Prioritize–what has to be done immediately?

Whatever the strategy that works best for the student, he needs to be wise about its implementation. According to the University of Florida researchers, students should be "Be Smart" about their strategies citing the following example (University of Florida Counciling Center, 2016). If I gave you a chalk and asked you to jump as high as possible and mark the location, would you jump nonstop for 1 day or plan your jumps to maximize your potential to reach the highest mark? The first strategy produces quick fatigue and limited improvement while the second strategy insures continuous improvement, working better not harder to produce the best results.

Not everyone responds physically or emotionally in the same manner to stress. Key to managing stress is recognizing its manifestations in a proactive manner. When one realizes, anticipates, and plans for a challenging situation or stressor, it is easier to manage when it arrives. As many a coach will tell, the best defense is a good offense; semester exams are no exception.

Demystifying Differentiation

In the Fall of 2015, over 50 million students were enrolled in schools for elementary and secondary education in the United States; this is according to the National Center for Educational Statistics (nces.ed.gov, n.d.). Of that number, over 12% were Students with Disabilities. Furthermore, 6% to 10% of the total number of students attending K-12 schools qualify as gifted (National Association for Gifted Children, n.d.). Based on this data alone, clearly, a one-size-fits-all instructional delivery model will not work.

Differentiation expert Dr. Carol Ann Tomlinson reminds teachers that teaching strategies are simply a "means to an end," designed to help students learn best. It looks at "who, where, what, and how" teaching is done and constantly looks for ways to improve (Tomlinson, 2014). Summing up the differentiation protocol details a variety of questions to help teachers focus on how to best maximize student learning (Imbeau, n.d.). The first step is asking "Who Do You Teach?" Naturally, using the same tired lesson plans and worksheets each year will not fit this bill. Step two is "Where Do You Teach?" Effective classroom teachers constantly "check the weather" to ensure that the learning environment is productive. Step three is "What Do You Teach?" What do the students absolutely have to master before leaving the

class, and how will they learn it? Some refer to these list as SWBAT or "Students Will Be Able To" lists. Step four, the final step, is "How Do You Teach?" Effective differentiation strategies include things like learning centers, learning contracts, and tiered assignments, allowing the learner to take an active role in his learning rather than to sit as a passive sponge absorbing as best he can.

TeachHUB.com recommends teachers ask themselves, "Would I like being a student in my own classroom?" (Ripp, 2012). By reversing the paradigm, and reflecting on what happens not as an instructor but as a student, allows teachers to readily see opportunities for improvement. These improvements have to happen in situ as the students have no active control on the involvement or lack of involvement of their parents toward enhancing their academic careers. Further as Lisa Mims, in her article "Teacher Reminder: Students Didn't Choose Their Parents" shares, "They did not choose their parents or their genetic pool. They couldn't say I want two college-educated parents who love me, care for me, and make my education a priority" (Mims, n.d.).

Differentiation is, quite simply, a multifaceted tool used by effective practitioners to enhance their students' chance of success by adjusting both the mode of instructional delivery as well as the practice of embedding the knowledge and skills in a way that individual students will most likely process and learn critical content in a manner relevant and consistent with their learning style. By beginning with the end of student learning in mind, effective teachers use differentiation to ensure that their students are receiving the quality education necessary to prepare them for the next steps in their learning journey.

The Real Impact of High School Students Who Work

A visit to a grocery store, fast-food restaurant, or retail store supports the realization that significant numbers of teens work regular jobs, in addition to attending high school. According to collaborative research published by *Developmental Psychology*, nearly 70% of high school 12th-graders work at some time during the year. Advocates of students working during high school cite "responsibility, punctuality, and reliability, character, and self-confidence" as by-products of working. Critics, however, claim that such work does not effectively educate or truly prepare students for adult employment and hinders academic performance in school (Bachman, Staff, PatrickO'Malley, Schulenberg, & Freedman-Doan, 2011).

The reality appears to be that students who work do have a "slightly lower" grade point average, depending on the type of job they hold and the hours they work. Students working intensely (more than 20 hours per week) while in high school are less likely to attend college and/or complete a degree within a traditional

timeline. Furthermore, students experiencing poor grades often see the lack of academic success as a reinforcement for increased loyalty to their jobs, unaware that the excessive working hours directly contribute to the lack of academic performance in school. Furthermore, University of Michigan researchers Valerie Lee and David Burkham detail how students who work intensely often begin a process of disengaging from school in academic work as well as extracurricular activities in order to focus more on work, exacerbating the isolation they begin to recognize in school (Lee & Burkham, 2000).

According to these researchers, excessive working during high school provides students with risk factors not only leading to a decrease in likelihood of attending college but an increase in the likelihood of dropping out of high school entirely. The risk factors are grouped into two categories, social risk and academic risk. Social risk includes a variety of factors such as low-income family status, family structure, school difficulties, and identification with a minority race. Academic risk, on the other hand, refers to students' behaviors and performance in school. Students who eventually drop out are often those for whom absenteeism and grade performance have been problematic.

This results in overall decreased academic performance in high school which directly translates to decreased postsecondary opportunities and outcomes. While the concept of students working is not likely to disappear, perhaps realizing that his performance directly impacts his opportunities in postsecondary advancement may help parents understand that student work, when necessary, should be viewed as a supplement to his diet of regular, academic enrichment, not as the main entrée for future opportunities.

Pre-K for All

Much has been written regarding ROIs or Returns on Investments for postsecondary school. However, much more needs to be written to enunciate the ROI for quality preschool programs. According to U.S. News & World Report, the ROI for quality Pre-K is 10 dollars for every dollar invested (Potter, 2014). Furthermore, the Foundation for Child Development details an analysis of 84 preschool programs, demonstrating that children attending Pre-K gained about one-third of a year learning benefits across "language, reading and math skills" (Yoshikawa & Weiland, 2013). Furthermore, from a societal impact, Pre-K programs are credited with a reduction in future crime incidences.

When evaluating the brutal facts, need vs. cost, one must often decide whether the costs are mutually beneficial for all children or more reasonably set for only those most at-risk, based on socioeconomic status. In "Why All Children Benefit from Pre-K," the PEW Charitable Trusts cites data where middle income children are often beginning school without the "social and academic skills" necessary for

success in an academic setting (Pew Charitable Trusts, 2005). They report that 49% of children unable to recognize their letters in kindergarten are middle income or higher, resulting in up to 12% of these children repeating a grade or dropping out of school.

While detailed, this longitudinal data indicates that both low and middle-income students benefit from high-quality "public" preschool, Potter's report shows that more than half of low-income 3-year-olds and a third of low-income 4-year-olds do not attend any form of preschool. Even among families making $50 to $60 thousand per year, only 64% of 4-year-olds attended preschool. Research by the Pew Charitable Trust has left little doubt that high-quality Pre-K enhances a child's chance of becoming successful in school and even later, in life. "They are also less likely to be retained, need special education support, and are more likely to graduate from high school. They have elevated earnings as adults and are less likely to be dependent on welfare or become involved with law enforcement."

The benefits continue, reports the Foundation for Child Development, when children have access to a second year of preschool with the most critical aspects of quality being "stimulating and supportive interactions between teachers and children and effective use of curricula" (Yoshikawa. , et al., n.d.) Clearly, Pre-K can no longer be considered a delicacy only for the high-income families or those with children needing special programming. Pre-K is critical not as a kick-start to a productive and on-target K-12 educational experience but rather to as a leveraging tool to ensure that children from all backgrounds acquire the skills to maximize their success, in academia as well as the world of work. The starting-line no longer begins upon high school graduation, it starts when parents recognize and demand quality Pre-K programming for all.

Reaching for Rigor

High school students have a variety of choices when it comes to selecting facets of rigor within their curriculum. In addition to what is considered the basics, or the minimum requirements for graduation, students have a cafeteria of choices from a variety of menus, depending on their school offerings. The most notable programs which offer college credit include Advanced Placement (AP) courses, an International Baccalaureate (IB) program, and Dual Credit.

While both AP and IB programs allow successful students the opportunity to earn college credit, they have dramatically different objectives. According to "What's Better for You: AP or IB?" (Edwards, 2015). AP was developed in the United States in order to "help students prepare for college." Students can take from a single course to in excess of 10 courses, depending on the opportunities provided by their schools and the level of commitment they are willing to make. IB was created in Switzerland as an internationally recognized diploma.

Dual enrollment is another option which affords college-level courses to high school students, allowing them to meet high school requirements while earning college credit. The most dramatic difference between dual enrollment versus AP or IB is the variance with which the program is offered. The National Conference of State Legislators (NCSL) on "Accelerated Learning Options" details how dual credit may be taught by high school instructors, college professors, or adjunct instructors with program delivery occurring on the high school campus, the university or community college campus or by distance education (National Conference of State Legislators, 2014).

With over 2 million students having taken AP exams in 2014 and 135,000 taken IB programs in the United States, NCSL indicates that a number of states have taken steps to invest in program support to produce students who are better prepared for college and therefore, perform better and maintain higher college graduation rates.

While there is no perfect program, Advanced Placement offers 38 different courses annually (apstudent.collegeboard.com, n.d.). The International Baccalaureate program entails rigor in each of five, defined categories (International Baccalaureate Program, n.d.). Dual Credit provides credit in collaboration with community college or university programs, depending on the agreement between the local district and the higher educational institution. Each program offers a number of benefits to high school scholars looking to enhance their competitive edge when applying to postsecondary institutions. It also allows them to expand their intellectual capital during their high school years, laying the groundwork for a most successful college experience and a productive and enjoyable future.

Apples to Apples?

An apple for the teacher is a frequent visualization when one imagines schools in the United States. However, amid the current, national political climate, one can easily become confused as to the value of the apples or, more specifically, the value of the education afforded to the children in the system. Even a cursory review of the national website on census data, census.gov provides the reader with some most confusing and concerning data on school funding streams throughout the United States.

Data show a wide range of spending allocations, depending on the state in which children attending public schools reside. For example, the highest per pupil expenditures can be found in New York, Alaska, and the District of Columbia with 19.8, 18.1, and 17.9 thousand spent, on average, for each child attending school in these areas each year. Conversely, the least spending allocations are found in Mississippi, Oklahoma, and Arizona with an average of 8.1, 7.6, and 7.2 thousand spent for each child attending public school in these states. An average of the highest spending allocations compared to the lowest spending allocations reveal that the highest funded states afford students nearly 2.5 times the financial benefit of those in the lowest funded states (Census Bureau, 2015). Amazingly, these students are all held to the same academic competencies both through standardized testing as well as college entry considerations.

The question that is often belabored, legislatively and politically, is how one is to level the playing field in such a way that funding equality and, therefore, educational equality can be realized. Given that the Constitution gives responsibility for education to each of the states, individually, leveling this funding formula becomes more complex. Federal funding is adjusted directly, according to the individual district's poverty, measured most often by Free and Reduced Lunch indices. Basically, the more at risk, AKA the higher the poverty, a district presents, the more federal funds it will be allocated. However, even with these supplemental funds, impoverished districts, especially impoverished districts in impoverished states, often find themselves facing an "Against All Odds" situation.

Schools allocated the least funding are not managed nor staffed by professionals any less concerned about the educational well-being of their students. They are, however, faced with a much more multifaceted task than those educators in heavily funded districts. They are expected to prepare students from less-prepared and supported backgrounds to be college and career ready with fewer resources both in the classroom and out. Much like expecting one to spin straw into gold, Rumpelstiltskin-like edicts issued whereby local educators are to produce golden academic outcomes without the power to purchase the resources, will likely generate a frustration similar to the one this fairy tale character experienced when he stomped himself into the earth. While funding alone does not guarantee educational excellence, the absence of adequate funding certainly limits educators' toolkits when it comes to facilitating learning outcomes which will give the students the opportunity to go forward to earn the gold.

Classroom Management 101

When faced with a classroom of students, teachers must establish clear procedures and rules of order to maintain a productive learning environment. However, an excessively orderly environment can actually stifle or even invoke student misbehavior due to its restrictive and institutional limitations. According to Eric Toshalis' "Five Practices that Provoke Misbehavior," negative student behavior serves as a form of communication. He explains that students typically demonstrate negative behaviors when they feel "vulnerable, misunderstood, humiliated, or betrayed." Invoking strict or stifling limitations on their already stressful environment simply ensures that Newton's Third Law will be carried out. For every action, there is an equal and opposite reaction. For students in a stressful situation, their modus operandi for reacting is to misbehave as outrageously as necessary to get themselves out of that most uncomfortable classroom setting. There are five provocations that every teacher should especially avoid (Toshalis, 2015).

- Highlighting ability differences
- Grading practice work
- Establishing vague norms
- Letting students choose their seats
- Using tired, old script

Whether intentional or unintentional, posting select student work highlights academic gaps. Grading practice work penalizes emerging learners and frustrates them to continue and continues to reinforce students for whom the content comes more easily. Establishing vague norms is, perhaps, one of the most challenging problems for students. Goals and objectives must be clarified very early in the instructional model or students are likely to achieve much lower feedback than deserved. Letting students choose their own seats may seem like a good way to avoid having to develop a seating chart and a positive step toward student independence. However, one must realize that students who broadcast the need to sit toward certain students are also flaunting their choices to avoid sitting by others. Allowing this practice assures classroom disharmony and isolation from day one. Finally, using tired, old scripts and dialog is sure to close the door to good student relationships. Sarcasm has no place in the classroom by students or teachers.

One of the best ways to mitigate negative classroom behaviors is to proactively manage the setting in a manner that encourages learning and establishes a safe environment for actively processing content. Without question, one of the most powerful tools to negate unwanted behaviors in an academic setting is to provide "praise and other positive interactions between teacher and student" (interventioncentral.org, n.d.). A goal should be to engage in three to four positive interactions with students for each reprimand given. This practice allows the students to understand that they are welcome in class while the challenging behaviors are not.

Senioritis, Fact or Fiction

If the temperatures have begun to rise, the days are a little longer and the foliage is in bloom, then spring must be just around the corner. For individuals outside of the K-12 realm, all likely appears to go on as before the season changed, just more fragrant, colorful, and enjoyable. However, for those individuals called to work with high school students, an entirely different transformation is in full swing. It is a condition which causes distress for a few students for the first time after Thanksgiving break and then goes into remission for a few weeks. Then another, less subtle set of cases are revealed just before Christmas. Now, by Spring Break, the condition grows exponentially, releasing an epidemic upon high schools across the nation. The condition is Senioritis.

Conditions are ideal for Senioritis when the pinnacle of the students' K-12 education is visibly drawing to a close. Graduation announcements have been ordered. Portraits have been taken, and only one set of final exams separate the students from their mirage of freedom. The only known treatment to ameliorate

the condition is to graduate them early. However, in most instances this maneuver is less than ideal. That leaves 9 to 10 weeks in which teachers, administrators, not to mention the cooks, and bus drivers have to deal with the side effects of students with Senioritis. Senioritis causes students to become unusually rowdy, disruptive, or just downright bizarre. They are either so excited to leave or so scared to leave that they demonstrate behaviors entirely atypical of their school career. As if the rules already fail to apply to them, one may catch an honors student willfully missing class or a star player feeling too important to show up to just another mundane practice.

Before everyone engages in a stampede to the guidance counselor's office to demand an academic exorcism of these formerly idyllic students, it is important that adults recognize the actual illness rather than simply try to treat the symptoms. There is a deep, underlying cause. The students have been held basically captive for some 13 years. Every decision was made for them. When to show up, where to show up, how to get there, when and where to eat, what to eat, and when to leave. All of a sudden, it's almost over. For years, the lectures and lessons have gone on ad infinitum. Who knew it would end so soon? One moment they were in kindergarten dressing up for Career Day, and now they are faced with actually beginning the preparations for that career they may have so long ago selected. There are no take-backs, no do-overs. This is real and it's coming fast.

The only cure is to graduate and take the next step. Once supportive adults come to recognize the illness for what it truly is, the better they can help equip affected Seniors to "boldly go where they have never gone before," to college, vocational school, the military, or the world of work. Fortunately, Senioritis, while a somewhat difficult condition to manage, if caught early, rarely results in long-term side effects.

STEM Growth

Early in their academic careers, students must select an emphasis on which they will build their intellectual platform. As soon as middle school, it becomes paramount for students to select courses which will effectively blend into their transcript matrix for effective and targeted high school success. In other words, if they don't take the most rigorous courses, typically math and science at this level, they limit their high school rigor index. A limited high school index lowers the ceiling on one's college options. Nowhere do these secondary limits become more transparent than in university settings, where 38% of STEM (science, technology, engineering or math) majors are unable to graduate with a STEM degree (National Math + Science Initiative, n.d.).

Careful not to blame the victims, one must also realize that based on nationwide data, only 44% of 2013 high school graduates were ready for college-level mathematics. Similarly, only 36% of these graduates were ready for college-level science coursework (National Math + Science Initiative, n.d.). Many of the students not ready for these STEM disciplines are not prepared simply because they were not deeply entrenched, early enough in their academic careers in K-12 to delve

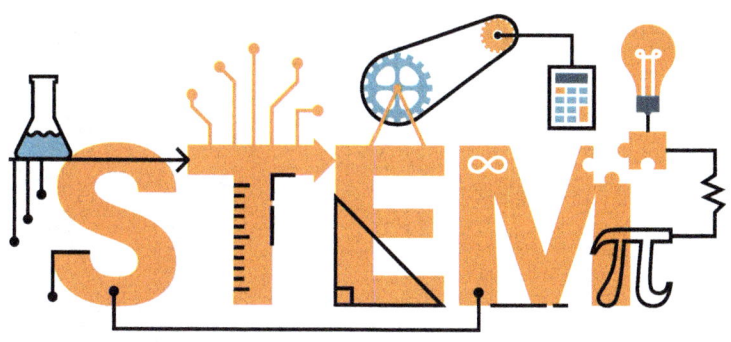

directly into the waters of collegiate math and science knowledge. Often times, overwhelmed by the drastic change in rigor, many exit stage left before realizing that they could, in fact, major in a STEM discipline, once they reach an acceptable level of academic preparedness. Much like learning to swim in a pool only provides the most fundamental understanding of swimming, then being thrown directly into the ocean leaves many heralding a life preserver and different, more tranquil waters. Direct entrenchment can be unreasonable without a focused and targeted mission for success in STEM.

In addition to being one of the most lucrative majors, STEM graduates are desperately needed throughout the world. Where many other majors find themselves facing a job market oversaturated by graduates, STEM graduates often have their choice of career settings and locations. Specifically, in 2008 only 4% of Bachelor's degrees awarded in the United States were in engineering, while China awarded 31% of its graduate degrees in engineering. The outlying variable is the K-12 preparation received by students in these countries (National Math + Science Initiative, n.d.).

In order to better prepare students in the United States to effectively navigate the waters of STEM fields and to capitalize on the lifelong opportunities located therein, educators and parents alike must work to facilitate and plan for academic success early in students' intellectual careers. Early planning for the mission of a STEM major helps students ensure that they are equipped with the knowledge and skills necessary to navigate those difficult waters with the success of an aged sailor. Lack of preparedness, on the other hand, rarely affords even the most talented, novice sailors the opportunity for a do-over.

Now You See Them. . .

The evolution of K-12 education in the United States is unmistakable. One-room schoolhouses were replaced by larger, more distinct classrooms and separate buildings set to house varying grade spans. This template has lasted the better part of 100 years. Now, however, in 2016, much like the Bob Dylan's song of the same title, "The Times They Are A Changin" (Dylan, 1963).

With the modernization of the world, we find a variety of challenges to the current K-12 structure where students are housed and maintained in an industrial-type setting. The first and perhaps most practical constraint is finance. Even a cursory review of current literature finds headlines like these: "Denver Public Schools to Cut 57 Positions" (Asman, 2016) and "No certainty that Kansas schools will open next year" (Williams, 2016). Rural school districts in states like Mississippi are attempting to shore the budget drains by consolidating districts. Even wealthy, urban districts like Boston Public Schools report trying to contend with a $50 million deficit (Fox, 2016).

These are real issues without simple solutions. One thing that is clear is that business as usual is not feasible for much longer in a large percentage of schools and states across the country. Discussions include shortening the school week to 4 days to save on transportation and utility costs, consolidation to maximize utilization of classroom space and minimize excess, school closings, restructuring, and tightening the budget. Often times, the only way to salvage special programs, that is, programs outside of the basics required for a standard diploma, is to look to alternative delivery. This alternative delivery may manifest in a community college, a university, or an online delivery mode to allow students to capture those essential courses and master those key skills necessary for their progression into higher education, vocation training or even the world of work. Without establishing a way to save these valuable assets, students are being set up for a most unfortunate outcome. Short of a budget windfall, something no one seems to anticipate, educational leaders have some very difficult decisions to make.

Furthermore, looking back will provide no benefit. Here we are. We are in many an aged structure with overcrowded conditions and an absence of funds to address the financial woes. This does not even mention the escalating academic outcomes demanded by federal legislators who expect more to be done with less and less. As Henry Ford is credited for saying, "If I gave the people what they wanted, I'd have given them a faster horse." The time has come in which educators and educational leaders and school boards must embrace a way to discover an alternative solution to the problem. Clearly, we are not getting any faster horses. The solution may lie in an entirely different delivery model, created to better educate tomorrow's leaders by using visionary thinking today. Public schools of brick and mortar, K-12, Monday-Friday, 36 weeks per year. Now you see them, now you don't.

Customer Service, P-12 Style

In order to provide the best consumer experience, a growing number of companies solicit feedback from their customers. Consumers have become acclimated to this kind of feedback mechanism from companies as omnipresent as Verizon, Starbucks, Toyota, and Shark Vacuums as it empowers them and validates their experiences. However, there is one environment which still seems resistant to regular customer feedback. The P-12 model in the United States was established with more of a focus on the ends justifying the means than on customer service.

Today's competitive environment is based on up-to-the-moment feedback from digital sources allows student customers and their parents to make choices. They may choose a specific teacher or choose a nonpublic school or select an out-of-district school or an online delivery model. Unlike years before, schools must be

very cognizant of their customer service image and consumer feedback messages. Whether solicited formally or informally, schools receive feedback. By ignoring the concept of customer service, one is certain to receive feedback in a manner that is widely disseminated and rarely positive. Prior to the digital age, frustrated students would air their ill will toward the institution using graffiti and negative student dialog. Since the advent of digital media, however, any given incident can be given a global platform.

As adults who lead and instruct scholastic institutions, it is often not a lack of empathy that leads to misunderstandings between students and faculty, rather it is a lack of clarity in the communication, resulting in oppositional viewpoints. Taking time to hear students' viewpoints, needs, and issues is a key first step toward establishing a culture of respect and understanding. When one is in line at fast food restaurant, it is very clear who is serving whom. Unfortunately, when adults become the workers, designed to serve minors, it is not entirely uncommon for them to shift the servitude toward career preservation rather than toward service to students.

Listening to customers can yield tremendous insight into their fears and needs. Understanding students' perceptions is key for educators to appreciate the tools needed to support their academic and social-emotional development. It is not the manner in which the feedback is gathered that is essential; it is, rather, the fact that the feedback is actually solicited and that the student customers have the opportunity to witness their voices having been heard that makes all the difference.

Leadership is accomplished through the consensus of the followership; good leaders know that listening is, perhaps, the single, most-empowering tool for shaping an organization's culture. The manner in which student customers rate and rank their schools may very well determine the success of that institution. Soliciting student feedback and responding to it in a proactive manner is more than a novel idea; it may very well be the key to the school's survival.

Out of the Box

The lazy days of summer will soon be a distant memory in the minds of children who have just gotten acclimated to sleeping in a little later and finding solace in some extra time for free play. School begins again.

Out of their boxes will come books, pencils and pens, and perhaps even some new shoes and a uniform top. However, the most important out-of-the-box selection this year doesn't come from a traditional, square receptacle purchased at a local store. It comes from encouraging students to think for themselves in a way that allows them to solve problems.

Thinking out of the box is simple. It means that the solution is only relevant if the student understands both how and why he reached the answer. It means that he has learned a concept well enough and individually enough that he can process the answer in a way that it is defensible and able to be duplicated with a similar outcome.

Unfortunately, many times students become compliance driven rather than results driven. Perhaps, this is because they sense the perception of urgency transmitted from nationally driven norms rather than the sense of calm from allowing for comprehension of content where they can understand and synthesize the *why* in order to develop the *how*. For example, solving a geometry problem without developing a proof (that series of steps which helps one justify his logic) robs the student of the latitude to explain how he learns. It is both unlikely and unreasonable to presume that all students learn at the same pace or following the same pattern. What they must do is eventually be able to arrive at the correct answer, consistently. While the path is immaterial, both the logic and the understanding are critical.

Without thinking out of the traditional box, we would never have realized personal computers, cell phones, digital media, smart televisions, replacement heart valves, laser surgery, or extended wear contact lenses. We are driven by limitless "what if's." That intellectual curiosity is what inspires us to create new and innovative products, tools, and concepts never found in that aged box of dated protocols.

It's time to be excited! School is about to begin again. It is time to welcome the innovative approaches to learning for understanding, to embrace the academic discourse, and challenge students to go as Star Trek advocates "where no one has gone before." Learning in the 21st century is truly an exciting adventure. Let us "live long and prosper" by nurturing our young academics to create a world where out-of-the-box thinking is advocated, and rote memorization for sake of compliance becomes a practice of the past. The success of society lies in the hands of its youth. Encourage, empower, and elevate their thinking to challenge stale norms and reach for the stars.

The Value of a Routine

As the alarms sound each morning, children and parents alike begrudgingly realize that it's time to rise and start the day. The difference between households where there is a morning routine and those in which a routine is lacking may very well determine the effectiveness with which children matriculate into the adult world of scheduled meetings, due dates, and deliverables. The truth is that few children leap from their beds excited to rise early and start another day filled with rules, restrictions, and rigor. However, it is this rule set that is the precursor for the formation of children's entry into adult society. The familiarity and pace with which they embrace the protocol may very well set them up for success or failure.

Effective mornings always start the night before, because nothing sets off a morning more chaotically than a child who did not get an adequate night's sleep. Setting out clothing, prepacking lunches, and stacking backpacks, jackets, and shoes by the exit are all key steps to an effective morning routine. Even setting out bowls and spoons and boxes of cereal can save valuable time in both the action of eating breakfast as well as the time often required to decide what one is to have for breakfast. While each of these steps may sound overly simplistic, it is these easy steps that ensure a child becomes acclimated to routine and predictability. It

provides him with both security as well as comfort to know what to expect each morning. It also provides one less stressor for the morning's activities.

As with any routine, the more one utilizes it, the easier it becomes. Having children help their parents create time-saving strategies is also a fun way to work collaboratively to get everyone out the door and off to school and work in as orderly a manner as possible. Distribution of tasks earlier is also key. Knowing who feeds the dog and who loads the dishes, in advance, avoids conflicts that can arise when everyone is frantically trying to get ready.

Using this collective solution idea, however, one must be prepared for some unique solutions. For example, sleeping in one's school clothes the night before or peeling the week's bananas in advance may not be the most ideal solutions. However, involving children in facilitating the morning routine is an excellent way to lead by example and help them set patterns that will follow them for life. Patterns of behavior help reduce stress and allow the family unit to work together in the mornings rather than create stress and havoc based on the lack of a preplanned departure.

These organized steps only take a few minutes the night before and dramatically help ease the morning stress. It is the rare family who cannot benefit from a few less moments of conflict at home before embracing the day and the potential chaos that it may provide.

The Ungraded Primary

Success or failure in school is quantified by a percentage and qualified with a grade to discern the comparative competency with which students' learning can be reflected by the assignments they were given. An "A," most would agree, means that the student has superior competency while a "C" reflects only moderate success. A "D" is barely passing, and an "F" is a failing, totally unsuccessful performance. For the likes of quantitative studies in advanced subjects like Calculus and Physics, few would argue that getting an answer correct versus incorrect best indicates his mastery of the subject matter. However, can one truly retrofit this linear thinking practice to a 5- or 6-year-old? For instance, exactly where does the "t" have to cross to be considered correct? Would it not be more logical to assess these developmental grades from a point of progress? Teaching is about establishing a culture of learning where various styles are encouraged and dialog is invited.

An ungraded primary concept is actively utilized in a number of school districts across the nation. Ungraded primaries, typically in grades K-3, allow children to learn and teachers to assess using their best practice tools and strategies to support a child's individual learning. An ungraded primary does not monopolize a teacher's time with focusing on grading reams of papers with a letter grade. Neither does it encourage instructors to administer scores of worksheets just to #1, keep the kids busy and #2, give the teacher something to grade and average with other assessments strictly for the report card. Unfortunately, K-3 students soon learn that a "D" warrants a frowny face. It makes the student feel bad about his progress and is a first step toward developing a negative impression of both his teacher and of school, in general.

In an ungraded primary, grades are more general and progress based. For example, they may be ranked according to levels of success for reading, such as "Developing," "In Progress," or "Mastery." While none of these identifiers tells the parent that the child is 88.8% in reading, each does give a much better feedback source for the parent. "In Progress," on the other hand tells the parent that the child is in-step with the curriculum and that no concerns are outstanding. Typically, with these types of "report cards," there will also be notations to the parent regarding specific standards which the child has strengths or weaknesses on which they can focus.

Teaching children to love school will never be accomplished by obscure quantifiers and frowny faces on papers. Taking a look at alternative approaches where learning is nurtured and a positive feedback system is established between practitioners and parents may be a good first step toward creating cultures of success in today's primary classrooms.

Lefties Unite

Based on a bevy of articles and Internet searches, one can reasonably conclude that only around 10% of the population is considered to be left handed. For over 90% of world, this is irrelevant. However, for the rest, it is a most significant issue. In schools, lefties encounter their first challenges. For example, markers, dry erase pens, and most of the ink pens tend to end up with more exudate on hands than the intended substrate. However, even as preschoolers, soon lefties begin to understand how to adapt to these bizarre products. They craft a way to hold the pen or marker in such a way that the excess ink is avoided. Granted, it does create a unique holding pattern, but necessity being the mother of invention, hold it they do. Further, students are often faced with desks designed for the vast majority of the population. Lefties have to sit sideways or nearly backward to try to make that bizarre "workstation" functional. Granted, there is occasionally an odd duck, left-handed chair available. If one is fortunate enough to get it, it's usually the one that has remained for the last 50 years and is missing many of its essential components as no one saw fit to maintain a seat that was rarely used.

Today's classrooms are also blessed with the advance of technology. Technology works beautifully if lefties are allowed to move that errantly placed mouse from

the right to the left. Yes, apparently, it very much does matter. Spiral notebooks are another piquant tool of antiquity for lefties. The spiral, positioned directly under the wrist, somehow has to be avoided at the same time they are trying to avoid smearing the ink on the tablet.

As lefties advance into adolescence and young adulthood, the world continues to provide challenges. Learning to drive a straight shift vehicle, for instance, is a feat requiring significantly more mental focus for lefties than their right counterparts. Much like speaking a second language, they have to tell their right hands how to maneuver the gear shift as if channeling to right had to understand what the left could orchestrate easily. However, amid all the obstacles tossed, they have continued to adapt. They have their own ball mitts and batting gloves, golf clubs, and guitars. Lefties cannot be "changed" to become righties. The mere mention of such an idea should be considered blasphemy. Imagine if Michael Angelo's mother had insisted that he use his right hand instead. The Sistine Chapel would be lacking a great deal of the detail it currently boats. Interestingly, lefties often lead. Given that five of the last seven Presidents of the United States were left handed (Sloan, 2012), clearly, they have overcome the backward world in which they live to not only survive, but to thrive. For educational practitioners everywhere, it is a challenge to *leftify* the classroom so that the students of all *handedness* are comfortable. Helping a lefty or two may allow them to avoid some of those challenges unrecognized by the right-handed culture, after all, they may just end up leading the world.

Farewell to the Bell

When one imagines the typical school day, it would not seem complete without the bells signaling that students need to advance to the next class session. This traditional form of nonverbal communication in schools is both effective and appropriate. One type of bell, however, needs to be reevaluated for its usefulness in classrooms; it is formally known as the Bell Curve.

The Bell Curve was once widely used to validate a *fair* distribution of grades. Within a normal population, students' abilities typically distribute themselves such that the majority aggregate toward the average or mean assessment. What becomes skewed in this application to a classroom setting are a series of complexities. A typical classroom of 25 students for whom the Bell Curve is applied ensures that some, likely 3 students, will fail each examination. Most practitioners would agree that 3 failures out of 25 would do little to support the impression that all students are learning at high levels.

While the majority of students should be successful in a given course if the instruction is effective and the students arrive with the background knowledge to proceed, applying the Bell in small populations can be both ineffective in validly representing student comprehension, resulting in administrative pressure on instructors to weaken the curriculum to ensure that all students appear successful. Unfortunately, this does not solve a paramount problem in education. A portion of students often need the opportunity to have the materials revisited, clarified, and reiterated. Typically, these are students who were unsuccessful in attaining mastery in a precursor course, although they received a passing grade.

Too often, students who are unable to process a given content set simply need the opportunity to have the skills introduced at an alternative pace or in a different setting to ensure that they are able to grasp, process, and retain the skills. Sometimes this is as straightforward as providing tutoring services by an educator. Occasionally, students will respond better to a peer tutor who can more effectively translate the content into *student speak,* allowing the students to relate to the content within their own narrative.

Assessments should simply be the tool used to evaluate the degree to which learning occurred not as a manner in which to segment the population into those who can and those cannot. Students should always have the opportunity to receive feedback and clarity on their work in order to understand how to improve their learning outcomes. Failure without the opportunity to improve only begets failure. Failure followed by reteaching and reevaluation is the only way to ensure that content mastery is truly an option for all.

It is long past time for practitioners, administrators, and legislators to stop analyzing the data as it applies to the Bell, and begin focusing on ways to maximize improved student learning outcomes for the benefit of the students, the community, and society as a whole.

Learning from Lexiles

Educational experts agree that reading is key to a child's learning. However, not all children read alike. Within any random class of 8th graders, for example, one will find a variety of reading levels. In order for a student to maximize his learning, he must be able to read the material and process the subtleties and inferences presented within the narrative. In order to best understand where individual students are reading, the most common tool used a Lexile measure.

A Lexile measure is a value which pairs readers with their appropriate narrative level (lexile.com, n.d.) and aligns with thousands of books and millions of articles. While there is no direct correlation between a Lexile level and a specific grade level, there are ranges of what would be considered on-target for 5th grade, for example. The Lexile reader score determines where a reader's ability is on the Lexile scale with ranges from 0 to 2000. A student's Lexile level is determined by having him take a test of reading comprehension, the feedback of which provides

a Lexile reader score. The lower the score, the lower the reading level at that point. Naturally, the objective is to take readers where they are and maximize their learning skills such that they continue to climb the Lexile scale.

Once a child's Lexile level is known, it is much easier to target ideal ranges of books or passages for him to read. However, it is key to mention that the Lexile level of a book, while it may be within a student's range of comprehension, does not mean that the content is suitable for the child. The Lexile level of a book refers only to the difficulty of the texts. MetaMetrics cites a child's range to be considered a "sweet spot" for his reading comprehension, but for educators not to be afraid to stretch a child's comprehension or allow him to read something at a lower level for leisure (MetaMetrics, n.d.). To fully understand the goal of Lexile, one must appreciate that an individual with a 700 Lexile or 700L is expected to be able to ready a passage of a similar level with 75% comprehension.

Understanding Lexile levels also benefits teachers within the classroom. For example, Sandra Bennett from Culpepper County High School in Virginia recalls her realization that she was creating a comprehension issue within her laboratory assignments. "I could not understand why my students were struggling so much with pre-lab questions. Once I realized that I was writing on a 1700L while my students were comprehending on a 1000L, the problem was immediately obvious." Detailed information can be found at www.Lexile.com. Lexile measures for books can be found at www.Lexile.com/booksearch.

To Friend or Not to Friend

With the omnipresence of social media, it is clear that some previously established boundaries between professional and personal spaces have been breached. In years past, a child's teacher was available by calling the school during her planning period or scheduling a meeting before or after school. Feedback was shared via backpack messenger not Facebook messenger, and there was a time delay between message sent and message received. Today, however, communication between educational professionals and parents and sometimes even students has reached an all-time peak.

While this can be construed as a positive interaction, allowing information to be shared almost instantaneously in order for parents and educators to communicate freely, this also harbors some hidden challenges. For example, many parents, and even some students, regularly engage in "friending" the teacher. While at first glance this may seem like a harmless endeavor, just the request, in and of itself, crosses the line between professional and personal. Now the educator is faced with a dilemma. Should she accept all parent requests, select requests, or none of them? Should she explain to parents and students at orientation that she prefers to

keep her personal life separate from her professional space and alienate an entire population of clients? Certainly, the more intimate and casual the parents consider the relationship between themselves and the teacher, the more frequently they will contact her and, perhaps, even expect some special consideration. This challenge seems especially difficult for teachers who also were raised in the age of social media. As digital natives themselves, communicating on any platform outside of access to a WiFi signal is entirely foreign. Therefore, they must be especially cognizant of not only who they friend but what they share, even on sites they consider to be personal. It is paramount that any new educator fully evaluates what she shares, in any context that could be considered less than professional. Not only will such content limit her employer's interest in her portfolio, it will diminish her effectiveness and credibility to her students and parents alike.

The latest advice encourages educators to create a professional space, rather that's the class website or another social location in cyberspace, it allows the educator to establish communication threads with her parents and even with students in a controlled atmosphere with a professional tone. These tools allow the educator to send messages and class reminders through one-way communication to a phone or email supplied by the students or parents. It allows her to maintain communication with the class without wandering into the personal spaces of two-way chats with parents or students that, sometimes, can become problematic and difficult to mitigate once they are established. To friend or not to friend, is a question that should be established before that first request appears from one's professional community. By proactively setting professional boundaries, the educator can control not only the consistent dissemination of information from her student and parent community, she can also limit their interface with her personal profile, allowing her to enjoy a more delineated role as professional educator separate from her family and home environment.

Little Uniformity on Uniforms

In years past, the idea of school uniforms typically conveyed images of Catholic schools where simplicity and plaid skirts ruled the day. However, many things have changed since public schools were declared and legislated. Today, children of both genders and all ethnicities are entitled to what is legally referred to as FAPE, or Free and Appropriate Public Education. What has not changed, however, is the debate on whether or not uniforms actually improve the culture of the institution. Even a cursory investigation into the topic of school uniforms can quickly generate abundant statistics and expert opinions to support both sides of the argument.

Twenty years have passed since President Clinton's State of the Union speech where he referenced school uniforms in this passage, "If it means teenagers will stop killing each other over designer jackets, then our public schools should be able to require their students to wear school uniforms" (Clinton, 1996). Unfortunately, the presence of school uniform policies does not appear to have had a measurable

impact mitigating the school violence witnessed in the United States on what has become an unfathomably, regular basis.

Uniforms today are commonplace in many public and private schools across the nation. Whether or not they truly make a measurable impact on violence, there is little debate that educators must utilize any and all tools within their reach to attempt to reinforce a school climate and culture of safety and security. Perhaps, by decreasing the glaringly obvious discrepancies between the haves and the have nots apparel, one variable of the complex equation of financial inequality is solved. However, one must also realize that, as Newton's Third Law teaches, "for every action, there is an equal and opposite reaction" (Reference.com, n.d.). While uniforms may attempt to convey an illusion of homogeneity, the reality is that the equation is far from solved. As long as some children arrive at school on foot in tattered sneakers and others arrive by luxury automobile, clad in the finest designer footwear, uniformity will continue to be an unrealistic aspiration.

What is key to remember is that K-12 schools in the United States provide so much more than the educational opportunities for which they were intended. They provide meals, most feeding their populace both breakfast and lunch. They provide a safe harbor, security, and consistency. While no institution is ideal or its mission without fault, schools in the United States are using every tool within their grasp to attempt to level the playing field and provide an equal educational opportunity for all in a safe and secure environment. While uniforms' existence or absence in educational settings will likely be debated for years to come, their concept is an admirable attempt to convey that all children matter equally. It is a nonverbal cue to reinforce that every child has equal access to the educational reserves available without regard to his background, gender, ethnicity, or financial status.

Time on Task

Nothing like a little break from instruction to encourage the students to waver into the pitfall of free time when it should be class time. While it may seem like a good teaching practice to allow students to break from learning mode to relaxation mode during an instructional period, nothing could be further from the truth.

Good teaching means students are well engaged with the topic and actively learning. This doesn't mean that good teaching requires the teacher to do all the teaching or all the talking. It does require the teacher do all the set up to allow any number of learning platforms to transpire during the class time. Effective instruction requires teachers to present material in a number of formats often using a number of delivery styles. Within a given lecture, effective teaching practices require the instructor to use one of the best, most underutilized tools of the trade, the wait time. He asks a question of the class at large or even individually, and then, he waits. It's painful for that instructional expert not to jump ahead to the answer and the next point; however, it is CRUCIAL that he allows adequate wait time. Wait time

allows the students, novices to the content, to process not only the content but to frame their responses in a manner that minimizes the chance of embarrassment and maximizes their opportunity to prove a valuable member of the class community. Further, it provides the instructor with valuable feedback. Does his question elicit the response of a few dozen eager respondents, anxious to answer the question, or does it generate a deafening silence whereby no student dares make eye contact for fear of being called upon? Both of these responses are extremely helpful. In the first case, the instructor knows that the content is lending toward comprehension and perhaps, even mastery. In the second situation, he knows that, clearly, there is additional instructional work to be done.

In addition to lecture, time on task can include student presentations and group work on a designated project or problem. This allows the students to validate that they understand the content and can relay it in a manner that assures the instructor that they have gained not only a passing understanding whereby they can generate a best guess on a multiple choice test, but that they can, in fact, apply the knowledge gained in a productive manner. Further, as a teacher becomes more skilled in his trade, he is more likely to be able to relinquish the control of the classroom to allow for some degree of dynamic learning to ensure that many learning styles are acknowledged and nurtured.

Time on task is key in each type of instructional setting. What is not valuable is waste time or time off task whereby the students can talk quietly among themselves, off topic. Allowing time for questions is encouraged as a best practice to allow students to have the teacher reiterate a concept not fully comprehend during the first presentation. Any adjustment to the delivery mode tends to reap tremendous results on student learning. The primary driver, however, must be the instructor. If he continues to facilitate learning in what the students may construe as fun time, he is truly beginning to master the art of teaching.

Sedentary Secondary Schools

With the confluence of courses offered for secondary students, that is those in grades anywhere from 7 to 12, students today have so many choices in both required curricula as well as elective options. They are often set to choose a traditional, vocational, or pre-AP track as early as 7th grade with student differentiation in math, English, and foreign language options clearly delineated. As they matriculate into a fully formal high school setting, the options continue to expand. The docket of choices ranges from a variety of business courses in accounting to economics to finance, many of which carry their own built-in rigor strands, allowing some to be advanced and others more moderate. In addition to the regular track English, there are a variety of literature studies and writing options to fully allow a student to begin toward mastery. Mathematics has become its own language at this level and offerings are both vast as well as divergent. That discipline alone provides an almost overwhelming number of courses which many majors consider critical for success.

While the expanse of learning opportunities is certainly cause for celebration in the intellectual community, it also brings with it a set of stresses which are rarely alleviated by adding another advanced class. In order to remedy the 8 to 3 schedule which typically limits students to 6 periods of study offset by one physical education time, many schools have now lifted the PE requirement entirely from the high school setting, provided that they replace it with another academic course. Academic competition being as intense as it is, where there are a scores of students and limited scholarships, students clearly feel compelled to skip the opportunity to exercise in favor of upping the ante on their academic rigor portfolio.

Certainly, no one can fault a proactive academic for delving in deeper to fully access his advanced intellectual opportunities; however, one must also evaluate the benefit gained by encouraging students to participate in endeavors such as physical education or extracurricular pursuits where they learn a variety of skills and develop an enhanced value of self while simultaneously diminishing the health risks associated with long days of sitting in class followed by long nights of sitting at home to prepare for the next day's rigor. While there is no doubt that colleges and universities seek to find the strongest, most agile minds to afford scholarships and to populate their campuses, they are also seeking students who are well-rounded and offer a diversity to their applications outside of what can be found strictly on an academic basis.

Leadership, team building, and cooperative interactions can all be developed more fully when students are encouraged to participate in extracurricular pursuits. While these activities typically bring to mind the images of super athletes and team starters, they also include opportunities like mock trial, band, and theater. Collectively, these avenues have been established to allow students to construct a portfolio that is balanced, with the academic rigors and extracurricular pursuits which truly reflect their talents and interests. As a number of institutions evaluate candidates for a holistic goodness of fit, meaning academic, social and emotional acclimation, a strong extracurricular layer may often be the outlier that separates a successful portfolio from the rest of the pack.

Keeping Tabs

To find out how a child's day progressed in school, parents of the past had to rely on a couple of informational threads. First, they could ask their child, "How was your day?" That, more often than not, it resulted in the famous four letter word, "fine." Given that "fine" has limited feedback appeal, parents also, occasionally, had the opportunity to sign a note from the teacher which often put a little clarity into exactly what "fine" meant. Typically, it referenced an infraction and the repercussions for the incident and required the parent to give the mandatory signature as evidence of his reading and acknowledging the incident. Other than those tools, parents could pry a little deeper into the details on a certain assessment or outcome of an activity. However, this approach gleaned only the degree of insight that the child chose to provide.

Parents of today use an entirely different operating system than those of the 80s, for example. Parents today list their cell phone, work phone, and five emergency contact numbers on their child's contact form. They list the hospital of choice as well as who has permission to pick their child from school. As generous as they are to share this information, they are just as strong in their convictions to have unlimited access to their child's teacher. A lone note home to report an occasional misstep or the annual parent-teacher conference will not suffice as adequate feedback with today's parents.

Typically, the younger the child, the more frequent the feedback required. It is not unheard of for parents of primary school age children to receive daily feedback from their child's teacher. Many teachers post on social media or websites regularly in an attempt to maintain a strong tether between school and home environments. Most instructors see this as a proactive measure to encourage communication through the channels they dictate and try to avoid receiving 20 text messages daily asking for specific updates on academic and social interactions. There is also tremendous social pressure from other teachers and parents alike to "encourage" these primary school age teachers to regularly communicate. Rather through Facebook or Twitter or any number of other social outlets, the teachers who promote their classroom in this manner are much more likely to be considered effective and desirable for the next class of scholars. As with many such efforts, the perception often becomes the reality in the parents' minds.

Parents of middle and high school students tend to expect less of a social construct from their children's teachers. They require brief but almost instantaneous access from both an academic and a social platform. Regardless as to the school's development of a digital parent portal for academic outcomes, parents of adolescents often need to touch base. Given the pressures evolved from students' dependence on electronic access to all things digital, the parents have also acclimated to instantaneous responses. This access has become so pervasive that many schools and teachers alike have adopted feedback tools like AlertNow which notifies parents (or those they designate) whenever notable activities are approaching or specific needs need to be met. Perhaps a test is imminent or a lunch bill is due. No longer can schools rely on sending home a note with the child. If the institution wants to ensure parental action, they need to be able to validate the message's transmission.

Asking a child to share his day is a great way to solicit information. Sometimes, parents even find out relevant information. More often than not, however, the information for parents of the 21st century is relayed electronically, responded to electronically, and acted upon long before any crumpled note of old could have made it out of the backpack and onto the counter for review. In an ideal situation, this instantaneous feedback provides a vital communication link for parents and teachers alike. While this is an excellent way to communicate and disseminate information with speed and efficiency like none other, it does leave behind a few token sentiments.

For the dedicated educators out there who still choose to mail home the occasional handwritten sentiment about a child's academic progress or evidence of character development, these novel tokens have the power to move mountains.

Communicating with Today's Teen

While one can reach as far back as the days of Socrates for evidence of the communication breach between adolescents and adults, today's gap is the most complex yet witnessed. Adults and children within the same home environment typically would agree that they speak the same language; however, this is only true on the surface. The language in which they converse is based, ever so loosely, on the same precursor language, but the specifics of syntax and delivery method are dramatically different.

Today's parents were raised in homes where communication was shared in person as well as via telephone exchange–albeit through that age-old landline solidly affixed to the kitchen wall, and even in written form by letters and cards. While there certainly was an informal language register whereby less structured grammatical patterns were used, the formal register used was very clear. Since the dawn of the 21st century, each year has continued to build upon a register barely

recognizable to the nondigital natives. Facilitating this new, often acronym-driven language has been the nearly omnipresent age of digital access. While this access has allowed teens and young adults across a variety of cultures to communicate with each other on an almost code-like platform, it has also alienated a large sect of the adult population.

While confusing as it may be, clearly, it is time that the adults learn to understand this new, somewhat bizarre language in order to be able to breach the dialog barrier between generations. While teens are likely to be shocked or even terrified to learn that their parents are taking steps to "learn the lingo," it is a critical step toward ensuring that lines of communication remain open between families. Ignoring this digital divide and insisting that children communicate, instead, on an antiquated platform is a certain recipe for disaster.

Ironically, the navigators of this bizarre vernacular and instantaneous mode of transmission are often sitting close by in one's home. They are easily recognizable as the individuals whose heads are inclined and ear buds are in place, allowing them to interact more succinctly with their digital peers than their parents. They type with thumbs as rapid as hummingbird wings and share subtle but profound messages such as "*$", for Starbucks; "9", for parents watching; "99" for parents not watching; "!", for I have a comment; and "10Q", for thank you. The list of acronyms and codes is seemingly endless and compounds daily. There are a large majority of codes which refer to actions or comments of a register entirely too common or too vulgar to share in this format. However, they, too, are easily accessible with a cursory perusal of one's digital device.

Communicating with today's teens is a much more complex proposition than in years past; however, it is critical that parents acknowledge the digital divide and regularly engage in open dialog with their teens. Furthermore, parents can learn a lot from their children and may even learn to speak a new language, most importantly, "AAR ABC." Translated: At any rate, always be communicating."

Bibliography

Anderson-McNamee, J. K. (2010, March 16). *msuextension.org.*
Andruss, P. (n.d.). *collegeview.com.* Retrieved April 12, 2016
apstudent.collegeboard.com. (n.d.). Retrieved March 23, 2016
Asman, M. (2016, January 19). *chalkbeat.org.* Retrieved August 8, 2016
Bachman, J. G., Staff, G., O'Malley, P. M., Schulenberg, J. E., & Freedman-Doan, P. (2011, March). Twelfth-Grade Student Work Intensity Linked to Later Educational Attainment and Substance Abuse. *Developmental Psychology, 47*(2), 344–363.
Berwick, C. (2015, March 17). Zeroing Out Zero Tolerance. theatlantic.com.
Census Bureau. (2015, June 2). *census.gov.* Retrieved September 3, 2016
childtrends.org. (n.d.). Retrieved October 5, 2015, from www.childtrends.org
Clinton, W. J. (1996, June 23). William J. Clinton: State of the Union Address.
Dylan, B. (1963). The Times They Are A Changin' [Recorded by B. Dylan]. W. Bros.
dyslexia.yale.edu. (n.d.). Retrieved January 7, 2015
Edwards, H. (2015, April 1). What's Better for You: AP or IB? Retrieved from blog.prepscholar.com
Fabelo, T., Thompson, M. D., Plotkin, M., Carmichael, D., III, M. P., & Booth, E. A. (2011). *csgjusticecenter.org.*
Foekler, J. (2012, December 12). *collaborativeclassroom.org.* Retrieved January 17, 2015
Fox, J. (2016, January 12). *bostonglobe.com.* Retrieved August 1, 2016
Ginsburg, K. R. (2006). The Importance of Play in Promoting Healthy Child Development and Maintaining Strong Parent-Child Bond. NIEER.org.
Graue, M. E., & Smith, A. Z. (1996). *Pros and Cons of Holding Out.* Retrieved December 4, 2015, from wcer.wisc.edu.
Gray, P. (2008, November 19). *The Value of Play.*
Griffiths, L. (2013, August 21). *How Active Are Our Children?* (B. M. Journal, Ed.) Retrieved from bmjopen.bmj.com.
Guskey, T. (2004, October). Zero Alternatives. *Principal Leadership*, 49.
Imbeau, M. (n.d.). *teachhub.com.* Retrieved February 20, 2016
International Baccalaureate Program. (n.d.). *ibo.org.* Retrieved March 3, 2016, from ibo.org.
interventioncentral.org. (n.d.). Retrieved September 3, 2016, from interventioncentral.org.
Jenkins, J. (n.d.). *10 Things Parents Need to Know to Help a Struggling Reader.* (Y. C. Dyslexia, Ed.) Retrieved January 7, 2016, from dyslexia.yale.edu/PAR.
Kahn, S. (2015, October 1). "Interview of Sal Kahn." (B. Frezza, Interviewer)
Kensinger, E. A., & Payne, J. D. (2010, December 17). Sleep's Role in the Control of Emotional Episodic Memories. sciencedaily.com.

Lee, V., & Burkham, D. (2000). *Dropping Out of High School: The Role of School and Organization and Structure.* Manuscript, University of Michigan.

lexile.com. (n.d.). Retrieved October 3, 2015

MetaMetrics. (n.d.). Retrieved October 8, 2015, from metametricsinc.com.

Mims, L. (n.d.). *teachhub.com.* (teachhub.com, Editor) Retrieved March 5, 2016

Moore, K. A., Croan, T., & Wertheimer, R. F. (2003). *Attending Kindergarten Already Behind.* childtrends.org.

NACEP Conference Archives. (2013). nacep.org.

National Association for Gifted Children. (n.d.). *nagc.org.* (nagc.org, Editor) Retrieved February 8, 2016

National Conference of State Legislators. (2014, March 3). Retrieved February 2, 2012, from ncsi.org.

National Math + Science Initiative. (n.d.). *STEM Education Statistics.* Retrieved September 18, 2015, from nms.org.

National School Transportation Association. (2013). *The Yellow School Bus Industry.* nysbca.com.

nces.ed.gov. (n.d.). *nces.ed.gov.* Retrieved February 3, 2016

Pew Charitable Trusts. (2005, June 15). *Why All Children Benefit from Pre-K.* Retrieved October 2, 2015, from pewtrusts.org.

Philips, R. (2015, July 3). REM Sleep Critical for Young Brains; Medication Interferes. news.wsu.edu. Retrieved from news.wsu.edu.

Potter, H. (2014). *PreK is Good, But Universal Pre-K is Better.* U.S. News & World Report, usnews.com/debate. U.S. News & World Report.

Reeves, D. B. (2004, December 4). The Case Against the Zero. *86*(4), 324–325. Retrieved February 14, 2016, from ccresa.org

Reference.com. (n.d.). *Reference.com.* Retrieved August 15, 2016

Reynolds, C. R., Skiba, R. J., Graham, S., Skaras, P., Conneley, J. C., & Garcia-Vazquez, E. (2008). *Are Zero Tolerance Policies Effective in Schools?* American Psychological Association. American Psychologist.

Ripp, P. (2012, August 12). *TeachHUB.com.* (TeachHUB.com, Editor) Retrieved March 4, 2016

Rosenberg, R. (2013, July 9). *Sleep and Childhood Brain Development.* Retrieved from everydayhealth.com.

Ross, B. (2010, May 26). 4 Days Work Weeks: Headed to Your District? education.com.

Salcman, J., & Shmeylovich, L. (2010, September 6). (J. West, Interviewer) edtech digest.

Sheehy, K. (2013, November 20). 4 Day Work Week: A Work in Progress. usnews.com.

Sloan, J. (2012, March 22). *disinfo.com.* Retrieved April 2, 2016

Snow, K. (2011, November 11). Research News You Can Use: Debunking the Play vs. Learning Dichotomy. naeyc.org.

Subramanran, R., Moreno, R., & Broomhead, S. (2013, July 20). *Recalibrating Justice.* Retrieved April 5, 2016, from vera.org.

Tomlinson, C. A. (2014). *Differentiated Classroom: Responding to the Needs of All Learners*. Alexandria, VA, USA: ASCD.

Toshalis, E. (2015, October 14). 5 Provocations that Every Teacher Should Avoid. *Educational Leadership, 73*(2), 34–40.

University of Florida Counciling Center. (2016, April 12). *counseling.ufl.edu*.

Wadley, A. (1974). *anitawadley.com*.

Williams, J. (2011, June 11). Redshirting: What's It All About?

Williams, M. R. (2016, March 8). *kansascity.com*. Retrieved August 22, 2016

Wright, S. (n.d.). *study.com*. (study.com, Ed.) Retrieved April 12, 2016

Yoshikawa, H., & Weiland, C. (2013, October 13). *Evidenced Based on Preschool*. Retrieved November 2, 2015, from fdc-us.org.

Yoshikawa, H., Weiland, C., Broook-Gunn, J., Burchinal, M. R., Espinosa, L. M., Gormley, W. T., . . . Zaslow, M. J. (n.d.). *fdc.us.org*. Retrieved November 2, 2015

Biography

Dr. Angela S. Farmer is an Assistant Professor in Educational Leadership for Mississippi State University. Before joining the ranks of academia, she enjoyed a career as a P-12 educational leader, serving the needs of children in public and private schools in the Midwest.

Dr. Farmer's research focuses on Leadership, Understanding Bullying, and Protecting Children from Predators. She is the coauthor of *Communicate Like a Pro* and has presented to international audiences on topics of Financial Solvency in Schools, Gifted Training for Global Learning, and MBTI Leadership. She holds a Doctorate in Educational Leadership from Oakland City University. Her Specialist, Master's, and Bachelor's degrees are from Murray State University.

Her vision for educational leadership is to treat other people's children with the respect and kindness that one would want for her own, in order to create a society of lifelong learners, armored with the capacity to embrace diversity of thought in order to improve the world for future generations.

CPSIA information can be obtained
at www.ICGtesting.com
Printed in the USA
LVOW02s0853270517
535637LV00002B/3/P